1 21 05

Hey Cowboy,

I remember back into
the 1950's. All kinds o
Animal Health Products were
into the market. Seemed like
products that always got results come fro
even today, want results. Get PHIZER

Keep Your Rope Coiled,

Ray

COWBOY POETRY
Of Legends Frozen in Time

BY RAY MEYERS

TATE PUBLISHING, LLC

Published in the United States of America

By TATE PUBLISHING, LLC

All rights reserved.
Do not duplicate without permission.

Book Design by TATE PUBLISHING, LLC.
Cover art painted by Tori Watson.

Printed in the United States of America by

TATE PUBLISHING, LLC

127 East Trade Center Terrace

Mustang, OK 73064

(888) 361-9473

Publisher's Cataloging in Publication

Meyers, Ray

Cowboy Poetry / Ray Meyers

Originally published in Mustang,OK:TATE PUBLISHING:2004

1. Poetry 2. Fiction - Western

ISBN 1-9331482-0-9

First Printing: December 2004

DEDICATION

This book is dedicated to those men and women who have so unselfishly sacrificed their time and their lives through the United States Military Services, that we might live in a land of freedom, security and peace.

Cowboy Poet,
Ray Meyers

FRONT COVER

The wooden wheels now stop, as the puffing team rests, on the crown of a snow-crested hill,

While resting they gaze fondly at the peaceful Coppage farm, warmly nestled in the valley below;

James waves to his daughters and wife, Harriet, Who are tending to this evening's chores:

His love for Harriet burns a flame in his heart that reflects the setting sun's golden glow.

Special acknowledgment to Tori Watson, cover artist.

TABLE OF CONTENTS

FOREWORD

Ray Meyers is a native resident of Roselle Township, in Carroll County, Iowa. The farm he grew up on raised registered Percheron horses and Shorthorn cattle. This farm was settled by Ray's grandfather, Christian, in 1867, and continued to grow under the Meyers brothers.

It was further developed by Ray's father, Rudolph.

Tractor power was becoming really popular during Ray's youth. Yet most of the work on the Meyers' farm was done by the huge, black Percheron horses. This provided Ray many a thrill in driving, riding, and training the fine, black Percherons raised on the Meyers' Farm.

At the age of eight, Ray went to the field with his own assigned team of grandmother Percheron horses hitched to a single row cultivator. Ray comments, "Those two old mares taught me more about life than I learned from all the rest of my formal educators—except one.

Throughout his youth, Ray had the opportunity to experience firsthand many hitching and driving configurations, including: Four Horse Up, Hitches; Four Horse Wide Hitches, and an eight horse hitch on a 3 bottom16" plow. Today, Ray and

his family continue the family heritage of Shorthorn cattle and training horses.

Ray acquired a cowboy's usual share of spills, runaways, and broken bones through his addiction to riding, roping, bulldogging, wild cow milking, bull riding, and breaking horses. Today, this cowboy poet, too old to enjoy a good bull ride, shares his life's experiences and adventures through his writings. Ray's favorite moments are found riding his faithful quarter horse, Johann, down a lonesome, dusty trail.

Ray has drawn upon his horse driving experiences, to relate to the reader what might have been experienced by the characters in this story. He spent many days researching the people, topography, and trails mentioned in this true story which is told as this author's opinion of what might have taken place.

Alise Meyers
Daughter of this Cowboy Poet

REMEMBERING THOSE . . .

OK, so you say you're busy,
But could you not stop to pray;
For that lonesome soldier fighting:
In desolate lands so far away.

They carry on in the harshest weather,
Seldom do they get much sleep;
And while you recline at your table of bounty:
Field rations is the meal that they reap.

Oh! You say, "God Bless America,"
But does it come from your deepest soul?
For we would not know the freedom we have:
But for that soldier who made our freedom his goal.

God Bless America!

PREFACE

Cowboy poetry is rhymed, metered verse written by someone who has lived a significant portion of his life in Western North American cattle culture. The verse reflects an intimate knowledge of that way of life and the community from which it maintains itself in tradition. Cowboy poetry may or may not, in fact, be anonymous in authorship, but must have qualities, content, and style that permit it to be accepted into the repertoire of the cultural community as reflecting that community's aesthetics in style, form, and content. The structural content of cowboy poetry has its antecedents in ballad-style of England and Appalachian South.

It is similar to popular works of authors such as Robert W. Service and Rudyard Kipling.

Credits to National Folk -life Heritage Foundation
Information taken from their website.

Some of the fictional characters in this book may at times display characteristics of behavior contrary to the values of our readers. I, the author, as well as the entire staff at Tate Publishing,

fully support good morals, good values, and wholesomeness of life. Anything contrary to those values is coincidental to the characters of the story and should not be taken out of that context. Different cultures have differing lifestyles.

While some of those lifestyles may seem offensive, care must be taken that we do not offend others for the beliefs and customs of their culture.

There are inferences of characters in this book using alcoholic drinks. Remember this was a time before over-the-counter medications. Whiskey was the cure-all medication. A drink of whiskey or brandy was, and is still today, used as a quick body warmer by people who have been out in the cold for long periods of time. The actual characters of this book were mostly of sound value; I by no means wish to infer anything less.

In God We Trust.

Of Legends in Frozen Time

Gidd—yap Little Roan—Take it on home Big Billy!
And the grossly unmatched team of horses lean into the load;
The fifth wheel front axel lashes the tongue wildly
between the two horses:
While the slow turning, wooden-spoke wheels rout
the rutty, rough road.

James Coppage had spent most of this day
cradling the long blades of grass,
That stiffly stood in the frozen sloughs of the
Brushy Creek's valley;
His day's salary of cradled bundles
now laded the wooden wheels:
The prized bundles numbered
thirty-four at last tally.

The rutted road rocking the wagon's bolster and load,
Nestles James Coppage into a deep, warm bed of hay;
His big frost-cracked fingers cling to the leather reins that guide
homeward his faithful team:
The horses' sudden quickened spirits,
now hint the near end of day.

The wooden wheels stop, as the puffing team rests, on the crown
of a snow-crested hill,
While resting James gazes fondly at the peaceful Coppage farm,
warmly nestled in the valley below;
James waves to his daughters and wife, Harriet, who are tending
to this evening's chores:
His love for Harriet burns a flame in his heart that reflects the
setting sun's golden glow.

Uncertainty it seemed was the only thing constant,
In an early Iowa settler's life;
Where the fickle Iowa weather, within a day's notice:
Could turn life unstable to strife.

Hillsdale is a German Catholic settlement,
On the east slope of Iowa's continental divide;
Where the watersheds of the Missouri and Mississippi:
Separate to once again coincide.

Hillsdale is a village comprised of farmers and tradesmen,
There are merchants, a few families, a priest;
These are settlers who traveled by wagon train:
From Ye old country, river towns, and back east.

These immigrant settlers build homes, barns, and fences,
These first years, how they slip by so fast;
Plowing sod, growing grain, raising herds and flocks:
A people united and producing the past.

The priest organizes workers and gathers up funds,
For the church that will yet come to be;
Reverend Henry Heimbucher comes from neighboring Mount
Carmel:
From ten miles north of Hillsdale travels he.

Reflective of small towns these people work together,
Like in this story where everyone is involved;
Yet how things happen and why? Some survive, others die:
These questions yet remain unresolved.

There is Franz Eshelbaker, and Anton Lawrence Horn,
Who with a four-up team of horses haul freight;
Like the teamsters of today, their travels flirt with harm's way"
As friends and family worry in wait.

Anton Horn is married to Catherine,
Home are two girls and their son;
Franz Eshelbaker is single and twenty-eight:
And a good catch for anyone.

There are the two, single German immigrant Bruner Brothers,
Wendlen must be about thirty-eight, Brother Lawrence is ten
years his younger;
From Germany they came to America's Midwest:
To satisfy their adventurous hunger.

There is Joe James from England and Joe Mathias of Ohio,
Who brought their families to till the rich soil;
And then there is Sam Todd, a bachelor, farmer, fur trapper:
Who could tell stories as others would toil.

Joe James is married to Cecelia,
They have three girls and three boys;
Joe Mathias and his wife, Mary:
Have a son and daughter to fulfill their joys.

Christopher Bussey came from Germany,
James Coppage from Virginia back east;
There is one old man, who has no name.
And the latest addition, a part-time neighboring priest.

Chris Bussey's wife's name is Rebecky,
They have two girls and a son;
A son and six daughters have the Coppage's:
James and Harriet live closely as one.

The farmer's winter harvest of slough hay, wood, and ice,
Is the reaping from nearby Brushy Creek;
Now the late winter weather, so fair and so mild:
Teases the promise of spring in a week.

The farmers order seeds on the threshold of spring,
They are delivered in the mild winter's retreat;
As a four-up team of horses reined by Eshelbaker and Horn:
Pull in a bobsled of seed oats and spring wheat.

Eshelbaker and Horn who haul in the seeds,
Run freight from their dock in Hillsdale;
They help neighbors on their farms, when not hauling freight.
Their big horses would pull through without fail.

A Meadowlark's song trills through the valley,
Snow melt droplets fill thirsting streams;
Sprouts of tall grasses great, the warm days of March:
And a Robin delivers spring's dreams.

On this threshold of spring—with supplies running low,
A supply run to Carroll is planned;
Should they travel by bobsled on remnant patches of snow?
Or use wheels to travel the land.

The plans are laid for the eight-mile supply trip,
To Carroll where there is coming a rail;
Nine men—three bobsleds—eight spring-fresh, shod horses:
Are chosen to bobsled the trail.

The Hillsdale residents share a restless night,
Anticipation and excitement run high;
The trip means perhaps fabric for that new dress or shirt:
Shoes that fit could now finally be nigh.

The villagers awaken at the first rooster crow,
Seems they have just settled down for the night;
The cows are milked early, pigs are fed, horses harnessed:
And breakfast is served at first light.

The sun on the horizon is two fingers high,
As the horses are hitched to their sled;
Last minute orders are given to the troupe:
As good wishes and farewells are said.

It's eighteen seventy, on Monday, March thirteen,
The troupe travels with weather so fair;
A small band of clouds rim the horizon northwest:
Hints of spring rains fairly fragrance the air.

The sled runners glide smoothly over fresh snow and slush,
Powerful horses are strutting their stuff;
Eight miles to town—load supplies—head back home:
This journey would be easy enough.

Geometric crystals of last evening's new fallen light snow,
Glisten like diamonds in the early sun's light;
They cling to the frailness of prairie grasses' brown stems:
And sieve through thatch to previous snowfalls of white.

Leading the convoy is Chris Bussey and James Coppage,
Driving Big Billy and the Little Roan Mare;
In the middle is Joe Mathias and his big team of Shires:
Each tugging to pull more than their share.

Joe James and Sam Todd team up with Joe Mathias,
Horn and Eshelbaker drive their big team of four;
On a triple box bobsled with a big team up front:
And a tongue team slightly huger than the fore.

Wendlen and Lawrence the Bruner Brothers,
Hitch a ride with Eshelbaker and Horn;
The single brothers, new arrivals, from their vatterland:
Of German heritage . . . ya . . . Vere dey born.

Wendlen said Lawrence, Des country eist grosser,
We travel weeks ust to get, vhere we are;
Des land est, ya . . . schon, Ve so much yet to see:
Vhere de land meets de sky eist so far.

Competition for power and speed among friends,
Has long been the American way;
There is a big team of Shires, Those unmatched Belgians:
And the four-up that could turn bobsled to sleigh.

But this competition involves more than speed,
More than endurance of muscle or will;
For the team that wins this homespun race:
Would be resultant of driver foresight and skill.

Joe Mathias and his Shires soon lost their lead,
To what appeared a-four-up, on a sleigh;
And these men did laugh, at the sight of James Coppage:
Who left the trail for the route's longer way.

Joe's big Shires were left miles behind,
When the four-up loped four miles of trail;
But as Joe descended the last hill to the slough:
Melted snow now covered the trail.

Anton Horn and Franz Eshelbaker, out maneuvered by James
Coppage,
Sat resting their big team of four;
Then heading their teams westward they circled the slough:
They had been outwitted by James Coppage once more.

Joe Mathias and Anton Horn are now walking their teams,
Circling the spring fresh waters of the slough;
Tall, brown prairie grasses softly bow to gentle winds:
It would be May before spring's greenness shown through.

One by one the settlers enter town,
Each tend to errands and go their own way;
Loading staples, buying shoes, dress material, and overalls:
Their tethered horses rhythmically chew stems of hay.

The men pass each other on the streets of Carroll,
Their eyes acknowledge who had won the race;
For refusing to speak of whom the winner was:
Saved the last man from a humbling disgrace.

Sam makes a visit to the cobbler,
Prices a tarp and purchases some traps;
Joe Mathias and Anton Horn buy harness parts and supplies:
And replace their worn out crupper straps.

About 11:45 at the Fourth Street Saloon,
They stop for a drink with the guys;
But no matter the conversation the topic would turn:
To concerns of the weird colored skies.

The sky turned greenish gray, with a strange sort of hue,
It is yellow—it is black—it is blue;
It is lightning; it is thunder, with a warm south wind:
Palm size snowflakes send folks running askew.

Spider lightning grows sharper, the thunder explodes,
Amid warm winds, huge snow flakes flew;
Joe Mathias looks at Sam Todd with a tremble in his voice:
He says "Sam our trip home's overdue."

Frightened teams break their ties, spooked horses mill together,
Colliding buggies with buckboards and sleighs;
A frightened team and wagon runs wildly through town:
Flattening anything that gets in the way.

James Coppage points to the northwest horizon,
He says, "Chris! L—lo—look—just over—there!"
In trembling voice he says, "Chris! Th—This doesn't look just
first class!"
And James Coppage didn't easily scare.

Quickly, Joe Mathias unties his team,
Those big Shires are full of jitters and sass;
Joe James and Sam Todd finish tarping the load:
This storm is just too big to pass.

Joe Mathias slaps his Shires and they trot out of town,
Crossing Raccoon River they're heading southwest;
Franz and the Bruners seem to lag behind:
Confident their four horses are best.

Anton and Franz now tarp their load,
Water their horses and feed them some grain;
They dig out their fur coats from the starboard storage box:
As wet snowflakes flutter midst plops rain.

Anton and Franz register with the census,
They are in no hurry to leave town this day;
Eventually, they found Wendlen and Lawrence the Bruner
Brothers:
And slowly, homeward, begin on their way.

"Why the big hurry?" Anton chided Franz,
"When we have this big hitch of four;
But Wendlen and Lawrence are scared out of their wits:
They'd seen storms, but not this big before.

Wendlen, said Lawrence, a nervous grin on his face,
As the brothers dive under the tarp;
"We cannot die now, and I cannot be an angel:"
"For I know not how to play that darned harp."

There are no noted landmarks between Carroll and Hillsdale,
No houses, no fences, no features;
Just the wide, rolling prairie. A blinding snow storm:
And the swishing tails of their hard-pulling creatures.

The trail to Hillsdale is hard enough to detect,
Through tall grasses during warm summer weeks;
The snow melting this morning has now filled the south slough:
And turned streams into flood-swollen creeks.

By the time the last sled has crossed the Raccoon River,
Northwest winds become biting and fierce;
Those big snowflakes split; into stinging arrows of sleet:
Shot from north winds so cold that they pierce.

Suddenly, so suddenly, temperatures drop,
The trotting horses even now start to shiver;
The sixty degree temperatures to sub-zero fall:
As Old Man Winter shoots stinging sleet from his quiver.

Joe Mathias and Joe James have now caught up to Coppage,
These were friends that Sam called Double Joes;
Sam's chiding and humor turns quickly to somber:
As the Temps dropped to zero and below.

Stinging arrows of sleet now join forces with soft snow,
Whipped by winds to a frigid whirling of white;
The big Shires stop. Their senses lost and confused:
By blinding whiteness, that likens darkness of night.

The white-out finally passes, some vision is regained,
The Coppage bobsled is nowhere to be found;
Though they're just a hundred feet to the left in this blizzard:
Void of vision, Void of tracks, Void of sound.

Chris Bussey and James Coppage continue on their way,
Ice covers their fur coats and thick beards;
Icicles tinkle on the Little Roan Mare's coat:
This storm had grown worse than was feared.

It's a teamsters rule to hitch the little horse left,
While the big horse is always hitched right;
But the horse named Big Billy had his own ideas:
And the hitching right was not Billy's delight.

Now who could believe the mismatch of a team,
Could determine a life or death fate;
But Billy's stride next to the Little Roan Mare's:
Curved their direction at a just perfect rate.

The wind-driven sleet stings the Little Roan Mare's face,
Snow crusts her back and her side;
She pushes into Billy to turn him downwind:
But Big Billy just keeps up his stride.

Chris Bussey and James Coppage can no longer see,
Snow and ice has frozen their face;
Hunkered down in the sled box, they are shielding their face:
But Big Billy just keeps up his pace.

James says to Chris, I think of my family,
Will ever I see them again?
James remembers that sunset scene from the hill,
All he treasures is back in that glen.

James treasures the memory of his six daughters and son,
Doing chores in that valley below,
And his heart feels the warmth of that setting sun;
Harriet's smile, and her—warm—loving—glow.

Chris peers out from behind his frozen hand,
In a wind's reprieve he glimpses Big Billy's tail;
But he sees it only in a fleeting glimpse:
Then it is white upon white and no trail.

Chris, in disparage, ties the lines to the stake,
Then falls back into the sled box with a shiver;
He prays, Lord, not my will, but Thine be done:
Now it's up to Billy and Little Roan to deliver.

Chris Bussey thinks of his loving wife, Rebecky,
His mind treasures its vision of her face;
He remembers his two daughters, his son, the good times:
And he longs for his Rebecky's embrace.

Meanwhile:

Sam Todd, Joe James, and Joe Mathias,
Are just a hundred or so feet to the right;
But who could detect them in the white, wailing wind's moan;
Or catch their breath in this dark swirling of white?

Joe Mathias says to Sam. "I know we're not lost,"
"But where we are, I'm just not really sure."
"By the direction of the wind, I think we're headed southwest."
"Question is, how long can we endure?"

With every passing second, the storm's fury grows,
Stronger winds, colder air, thicker snow;
By now, accumulation is sled runner deep:
And at least five more miles to go.

Sam Todd takes his turn at driving the Shires,
Dobbins and Nell are now nowhere in sight;
Sam said, I can feel them as they tug on the lines:
Sam just keeps the winds quartering their right.

Sam, Joe, and James want to get home really bad,
There are no landmarks in sight to be found;
The valleys are filled with over knee-deep snow:
The wind sweeps the hills bare to the ground.

Again Dobbins' rump is no where in sight,
Sam tugs the off-line like grim death;
Fighting to keep quartering the cold northwest wind:
Each man fights just to capture his breath.

Sam's arms are aching as he fights that off-line,
Dobbins and Nell take the storm in their flank;
Sam feels through the lines that they are climbing a hill:
When the sled nears upset in a bank.

The runners of the sled bump up on the right,
Sam Todd pulls the team to a halt;
The sled rocks and sways, Joe James falls overboard:
It's like riding the San Andreas Fault.

Joe Mathias jumps overboard to rescue Joe James,
They find each other by calling Joe's name;
They crawl aimlessly through the snow, which way should they
go:
Joe James shouts. "It's my fault! I'm to blame!"

Searching for the sled just twelve feet ahead,
They crawl about as young kids in white sand;
Gasping for breath as they crawl against the wind:
Then Joe Mathias feels something familiar in his hand.

It is hard, It is a rock, It's near as big as the sled,
It is black, and oh yes! There are more!
Then he laughs and he shouts, as he remembers those hot days:
Clearing land in the summer days of yore.

I know where we are! Shouts Joe Mathias,
These are the rocks that I cleared from this field!
We are two miles due north of Hillsdale! They rejoice.
As to the biting winds now they could yield.

Sam quires of Double Joes. Remember our friends?
Where are they? What of them has become?
They picture Bussy and Coppage with that odd, unmatched team;
But that team of four would be nice now Dad-Gum.

Meanwhile:

Anton and Franz have their hands full,
Their might is spent trying to guide those four horses;
For to quarter the wind with a team of four-up:
Is impossible with these velocity forces.

Anton's arms ache as he tensions the off-lines,
He tries to keep the sled headed southwest;
But two miles out of town the lead line gives a snap:
And a runaway ensued as you guessed.

The four horses are angered by the blinding snow,
By the sleet constantly stinging their face;
They're resentful of ice painfully pulling their hair:
Suddenly free now they set their own pace!

The freed horses go wild—they're headed due south,
Their pace likens a runaway lope;
Yet when the horses slow down, Anton urges them on.
To wear them down now was Anton's best hope.

Out of breath, the horses gradually slow down,
Yet they trot through the next mile of snow;
With the remaining three lines, Anton circles them left:
Through this wind the horses cannot hear whoa.

Franz says to Anton, Good driving my friend.
His words quiver from the chill of his shiver.
Anton replies, but I worry of our friends.
For their tracks turned due west at the river.

Meanwhile:

Sam Todd shouts above the wind. My shack's a mile south,
Then follow west the field border of tall weeds.
I tell you they are tall. If we find that field border.
I know to my home it proceeds.

The trio of farmers is now revived in hope.
The southbound Shires even quicken their walk.
Relieved of their tensions the men laugh and joke.
How of this venture they would so many times talk.

Forcefully, the storm pushes the team and sled south,
The storm laughs as the men enjoy their reprieve;
It pushes them onward to their next unknown fate:
This storm has an ace up his sleeve.

Now upon finding their fence row of tall weeds,
The trio turns their big Shires due west;
It is now perseverance. It is desire, and strength:
It is storm against man in a test.

The big team refuses to face the storm,
Storm and beast now put man to the test;
Several times they try to turn the big team to Todd's home.
But the team just refuses to go west.

Then shouts Joe Mathias. That sack of flour.
We can cut it and fashion a horse blind.
The horses' tensions are wound to the snapping point:
And their spring is about to unwind.

Double Joes fumble to open the sack,
White flour whirls away in a gust;
Before the flour sack into a blind can be fashioned:
It freezes stiffly to a hard board like crust.

Joe Mathias and Joe James now ill-tempered by this storm,
Each struggle to the fore of a horse;
They untie the hame straps encrusted in frozen snow:
"You drive Sam! We'll lead 'em by force!"

That field border of weeds, though tall and thick,
Does little to break the force of the storm;
A Joe leading each horse and Sam pulling the off-line:
Will they ever reach that cabin so warm?

The men struggle for balance in the waist deep snow,
They dream of that warm cabin fire;
Unable to breathe while facing the wind:
Would that warmth be their dying desire?

Take a step—pull the horse,
Take a step—pull the horse,
Take a breath—when you turn—from the wind:
Take a step—keep—your mind—on the course.

Follow the sequence—then do it again,
They continue for an hour of more;
Take—a—step, pull—the—horse:
Until Sam shouts. There's my cabin door!

All three fumble to unhitch the team from the sled,
The barn door is frozen shut with snow;
Somehow the horses are put up for the night:
Sam says. "There's whiskey in the house, shall we go?"

The exhausted men enter the cabin,
Through the windows and cracks sift the snow;
The cabin is cold, the fire is out.
Would this cold in their bones ever go?

With each gust of wind the cabin would shift,
The nails pull in the boards with a creak;
Sam said. "I just don't know—how long this shack can stand:"
"This wind has stressed the frame, and it's weak."

The three exhausted men pull themselves together,
Once again to do battle with the storm;
For with each creaking sway, the cabin would weaken:
If it went, they would never know warm.

Sam removes the gin pole from his hay wagon,
Double Joes find a tongue and small tree;
They brace up the lee-ward side of the cabin:
Now will it stay? They would just have to see.

Meanwhile:

Back to Chris Bussey and his friend James Coppage.
With Big Billy and the Roan Mare with no name.
The clock read about three in the afternoon:
But this loose team trods on just the same.

The Little Roan Mare has frozen her face,
This can happen though the chance is remote;
She is crusted with snow from her head to her sole:
With the harness froze tight to her coat.

Big Billy has his mind set—and it is home to his barn,
Each step toward that barn is a gain;
And the Little Roan Mare sets her heart to go on:
Though each step is a hair pulling pain.

The self-driven sled team, plods into Hillsdale,
It is a ghost town in a death shroud of white;
Just two miles to the barn, Billy quickens his pace:
Would he have them all home before night?

Hillsdale is a ghost town in a shroud of blinding white,
The men and sled unknowingly stealth through Hillsdale;
There are invisibly no people, no lights in the windows:
The huddled passengers only hear the wind's wail.

Plodding out of town, their slow pace reduces,
For on Billy the snow rises to knee-deep;
Billy is now pulling both sled and Roan Mare:
She is weakening. So her—pace—he will—keep.

James Coppage and Chris Bussey shiver under the tarp,
That covers the box of their sled;
Their clothes are frozen wet and both fight imminent sleep:
Both have the fear being found somewhere dead.

Their thoughts of grim death become a terror of mind,
Yet Billy plods through the deepening snow;
How will we be judged? Have we lived a good life?
Would it be Heaven or to Hell they would go?

Snow over his knees, yet Big Billy plods on,
Jerking the—sled as a—written—rhythmic—score;
Lulling James—and Chris—into the—warm sleep—of death:
The—sled jerks—and then—nothing—more . . .

James and Chris awaken to a light up above.
They hear their names, Oh please come to life!
Have they gone to Heaven? Or? No!—Could it be?
Yes, it's Harriet, James Coppage's wife!

Harriet and her girls are out doing chores,
Preparing for a long, deep, cold night;
When two horses and a bobsled approach the barn door:
But the little horse isn't roan! She is white!

James and Chris warm in the cabin by the fire,
Drying off and each soaking up heat;
They peel off wet clothes that are frozen to their skin:
And feel the painful blue toes on their feet.

Billy and Roan Mare are unhitched from the sled,
And well fed in their deep bedded stalls;
They spend this night with their harness frozen tight:
Snow sifts into the barn through the walls.

Harriet and her girls brush snow from the team,
To a half-inch of hair froze in ice;
Harness buckles and snaps are frozen solid with ice:
Locking the horses in a leather harness vice.

The Little Roan Mare sleeps well tonight,
It was such a challenging day;
She is thankful for Big Billy, who had led her home;
But Big Billy just munches his hay.

Two of the sled parties have made it safely home,
Though neither know the others good fate;
But where is the party of Anton and Franz?
Night lurks it is now getting late.

Meanwhile:

Anton and Franz have repaired the off-line,
Though now they are hopelessly lost;
They argue of being east or west of Hillsdale
Their faces frozen in ice, snow, and frost.

Sheltered by the tarp in the back of the sled,
Wendlen and Lawrence grow cold yet are dry;
They have no warm clothes, like Anton and Franz:
They give a frustrated, chilled, shivering sigh.

Anton reasons that in the runaway,
The horses ran away from the wind;
It would stand to logic they are now east of Hillsdale:
And that direction they would have to rescind.

Anton attempts driving his team due west,
Against cold wind, crusting snow, stinging sleet;
But the team pulls back south, Anton circles them around:
Several times then admits to defeat.

Then Franz in raging anger grabs the lines from Anton,
Slaps the horses and drives them due west;
The right leading horse bocks getting tangled in the harness:
But Franz knows that he's given it his best.

The lost bobsled travels a few miles more,
Sometimes south and sometimes southeast;
The drivers are delusional, they are wet; they are cold:
They hold the lines but just follow their beasts.

Frozen snow crusts the faces of the hardy, bearded teamsters,
Their conversation is a confusing angered tiff;
Their every move is restricted by ice-caked, board-stiff coats:
Driving lines fall from their hands frozen and stiff.

The horses plow over a snow-crested ridge,
There is shelter on the lee-sided hill;
They will go no further; this is camp for the night:
And their sled has upset on a rill:

The box has separated from the overturned sled,
To up-turned runners the four horses are tethered;
The overturned sled box will be their shelter tonight:
It is the best place for the storm to be weathered.

The box is stabilized in its upturned position,
The covering tarp becomes now the floor;
The usable supplies are packed into the shelter:
Through the end gate that now serves as the door.

Franz makes an oil lamp from a whiskey bottle and wick,
It would help but his wet matches don't light;
The four men have found shelter from the frigid and dark:
Yet winds howl through their silence of plight.

The Bruner Brothers huddle in under a heavy blanket,
That they fashion from sacks of sugar and flour;
The sack's weight is overwhelming, uncomfortable, yet warm:
They wait hour—after hour—after hour.

Franz finds a dry blanket that he spreads on the floor
Seeking warmth lying in wet clothes he curls;
Anton sits huddled on a flour sack by the door:
While outside snow voraciously whirls.

Huddling in cocoons the men's shivers now pass.
Though Anton and Franz are soaked wet to the skin;
Each thinks of their families, their loved ones, and friends:
How they'd change life if they lived it again.

Anton and Franz comment how stinging toes and fingers,
No longer hurt, and feel warm yet they're numb;
Anton rests his face in the cup of his hands:
His lips feeling the cold in his thumb.

Hours slowly pass, the men grow ever silent.
And pray that their soul He would keep;
Their minds wander as they sense, His Warming Light:
Then find warmth in the welcome of sleep.

Suddenly outside is a rumble,
Then a crack, and a horse's frightened neigh:
The storm's equine prisoners once tethered to sled runners:
Have broken free from the curse of their sleigh.

The horses are angered by the stinging sleet,
Their hair is pulled by the crust on their coat;
Their mind is crazed by the bitter cold:
Survival's chances grow dimly remote.

The tongue team leaves and heads due south,
Hitched together by the spread lines and yoke;
But the lead team separates and are headed for home:
With their harness mostly shredded and broke.

The tongue team travels about a mile south,
Seeking shelter from the storm's torment;
They circle as if driven on a familiar horse power:
Live horses with their brains frozen dormant.

Together the lead team heads for home,
Facing cold winds, they're blinded by snow;
They travel four miles before losing their senses;
Their direction and purpose to go.

The shelter they find from the bitter cold winds,
Is by Brushy Creek at farmer Cole's place;
Disoriented and tired the hungry team pace:
Gaunt shadows of this morning's sled race.

Meanwhile:

Outside of the sled box through the dark of the night,
Relentless winds continue their wail;
Anton envisions his young bride, Catherine:
"For love of her I must somehow prevail."

Anton fights sleeping through his semi-conscious state,
Then dozes into deepening slumber;
Gradually he feels warmth of death's sleep:
Then finds welcome in the spirit world's number.

The dark, cold night passes slowly into the blizzard's new day,
In the chilled sled box lurks darkness and death;
"Anton! Franz!"—Call Wendlen and Lawrence:
But—No reply—Not even a breath.

This overturned sled box. This shelter for life,
Becomes man's entrapment in the blizzard's cold womb;
Frightened: The Bruner Brothers try lifting the box,
Wendlen and Lawrence are now trapped in a tomb.

Fighting and struggling they try lifting the box,
Unwilling to accept death as their fate;
They try tipping the box over, but it will not move:
They've forgotten to use the end gate.

Remember the tarp is tied to the box,
Making the tarp the floor where they wait;
Thus lifting the box is like standing in a basket:
And with the handles try lifting their weight.

Wendlen and Lawrence finally grapple with their senses,
To get out they must open the end gate;
But who will be first to climb over those dead bodies?
"You go first Lawrence, Think I help, I wait."

Lawrence goes first, He climbs over Franz,
Franz's body lies curled—cold—and stiff;
Then he finds Anton, hands froze to his face:
If this end gate will open now—If?

With a rush of relief, the gate latch comes free,
Out pops Lawrence behind is his brother;
Both amazingly comment, as the storm rages on:
"Dese American storms dhey like not any odder."

Passing from the clutches of their would be coffin,
Into the grasp of the blizzard's torment;
The brothers must contend now with staying alive:
Or being found somewhere frozen stiff, cold, and dormant.

Direction turned and totally lost,
The Brothers drift with the wind-driven snow;
It's impossible to breathe while facing the storm.
So they drift the only way they can go.

Just ten steps they have gone, through waist deep snow,
Snow tangled with chest-high prairie grass;
They wade and crawl, then having given it their all.
They surrender to the storms deep impasse.

Literally, they swim through this ocean of deep snow,
Traveling a mile though it seems like much more;
They are weakened by hunger, their faces crusted in snow:
They tread an ocean of white with no shore.

"My feet, my hands," cried Lawrence, "Are numb!"
"And I'm hungry, and we've no food to eat!"
But their hope is renewed by the sight that they viewed.
In a moment of the blizzard's retreat.

Just fifty feet ahead through the waist deep snow,
Is a clearly marked wind-swept trail;
The snow is blown clear, and it follows a ridge:
We found the road that carries the mail!

Wendlen struggles—he crawls—he coaxes Lawrence on,
Till at last they reach the wind-swept path;
Then struggling brother Lawrence tries to walk on numb feet:
That froze last night, in the storms cold, bitter wrath.

Logic tells the brothers that this trail leads to home,
If they fight the winds in a head-on direction.
It's impossible to breathe while facing the wind;
Their coats offer very little storm protection.

Wendlen and Lawrence stumble down-wind,
Treading the trail as they're supporting each other;
Their faces and hands frozen. They walk on numb feet:
But their spirits warm by fleeting thoughts of their mother.

Wendlen continues—half carrying his brother,
Brother Lawrence falls into a semi-conscious sleep;
"Oh, keep going little brother. I can't carry you:"
"I'll find help Lawrence, Wendlen eyes start to weep."

Wendlen continues to follow the trail,
There are no landmarks, no features to read;
Just a trail on a ridge that is thirteen miles long:
That from Hillsdale to Carrollton would lead.

Wendlen stumbles; He falls to his face,
He is hungry. When last did he eat?
He struggles to stand. Then finds a walking stick:
It's like walking and having no feet.

Wendlen's senses are unclear, he's confused, and in tears,
His conscience professes its guilt;
He abandoned his dying brother. Brought him here to this land:
Now their fortunes, No way could be built.

Another mile passes, then another and more,
Wendlen moves on though it's hardly a walk;
It's the wind that pushes. It's his desire to find help:
His lips blister; his cold tongue cannot talk.

Wendlen falls, he thinks of his brother,
The warm hills of home tease at his mind;
He tries to crawl on, to find help for his brother:
His cold eyes are blurry and blind.

"I cannot forsake you, I love you my brother,"
Wendlen reaches and crawls down the road;
Though it's only a step. It's progress toward help:
He collapses from his cold body's load.

Then Wendlen awakes to the beauty of song,
There's a sled. There's Franz, Lawrence and Anton;
There are four silky white horses, a steep, narrow trail paved
gold:
Angels greet them, and urge them come—on!

Meanwhile:

Sam Todd, and Double Joes, huddle close to the fire,
Its four P.M. that very same day;
When suddenly, so suddenly, as the whole storm began:
The sun shines and fierce winds in peace lay.

Sam and Double Joes, hike immediately to Hillsdale,
The landscape is a sight to behold;
Ridge swept snows fill valleys to twenty-feet deep:
Sam's thermometer read minus thirty-five of cold.

One-by-one settlers dig free from the snow,
They assemble at the store in Hillsdale;
Chris Bussey and James Coppage made it home with some
struggle:
But the Horn family just grieve, morn, and wail.

Sam and Double Joes chide themselves with excuses,
Like the missing troop might have stayed back in town;
But try as they may, excuses don't work:
And the villagers return home feeling down.

It was early on Wednesday the Fifteenth of March,
Warm sun pierced the chilled air of dawn;
The farm chores were quickly finished, and the settlers
assembled:
Soon a party of searchers was spawn.

The Hillsdale search party covered many trails to Carroll,
Most rode horses as now sleds were too slow;
They were met by fifty townsmen and merchants from Carroll:
Riding south through hills and valleys of snow.

"How on earth did you survive? We thought you had perished."
Spoke the reporter from the Carroll Daily News.
Sam Todd proudly answered, recounting his experience,
And filling in the blanks with his views.

Just two miles east of Hillsdale a sled track was found,
Sled tracks frozen in the crusted hard snow;
The tracks led southeast, As though driven by the storm:
They were traced into a valley below.

Then a rider from the south alerted the search party,
"It's the craziest thing you will see;"
"I have found Anton's tongue team, walking circles in the snow:"
"They're brains are frozen. They're crazed as can be:"

The team's faces were frozen; their eyes turned to ice,
Their velvet noses are hard, cold, and blue.
Their ears frozen hard, all comprehension is gone:
To put them down was the kind thing to do

Now a saddened search party moves on in silence,
Hardened men bite their lips—grit their teeth;
For as a news man noted but never put it in print:
"Even tough men have a heart underneath."

About a mile north of where the horses were found,
The overturned bobsled is in snow buried deep;
When the snow is dug away, the end gate is opened:
To a grotesque sight that would haunt the men's sleep.

Anton Horn is seated by the end gate,
His hands folded, they cover his face;
Franz Eshelbacker is lying curled tightly on a blanket:
The smell of death emits from this place.

A sled takes the bodies back to Hillsdale,
The Bruner Brothers have yet to be found;
It's reasoned the winds would have taken them south:
To the mail route, on high wind-swept ground.

But some men argue, "They would have headed west,"
"To Hillsdale, In spite of the storm;"
"Think if it were you, would you not challenge the storm?"
"To get back to your home where it's warm?"

The search party splits up, some accompany the bodies,
Some go west through the sea of deep snow;
Still others go south as the wind would have forced them;
To the mail route, which way would you go?

The search party going west fatigued by deep snow,
Held in place by chest-high prairie grass;
Trail cutting horses bocked, but slowly on rode one man:
With his bay sixteen-hand-high jack a—.

Conversation continued, "Had the brothers come this way,
They could be buried in this ocean of white;"
"They could have passed through Hillsdale, unable to see:
Men to be sure, we'll ride west until night."

Meanwhile:

The search party going south, encountered the same,
Deep snow held in grass six-feet tall;
They continued south a mile, till the mail route was found:
They progressed slowly, yet sometimes not at all.

When searchers found the mail route. The trail was swept clear,
Save for frozen skiffs that the cold wind had made;
Then the frozen footprints of brothers walking southeast:
One was struggling, the other his aid.

The frozen footprints wobbled and weaved down the road,
Searchers followed them a good mile so it's said;
Until there on the road in foreseeable distance;
Lay Lawrence Bruner, His body frozen—stiff—dead.

A few of the searchers stay with the body,
Others pressed onward led by the next track;
One mile—Two miles—Three miles—Then:
Wendlen Bruner is found stiff, frozen black.

The brothers are carried up the trail to Hillsdale,
The toughened men bite their lips with a sigh;
But home in Hillsdale, Another scene takes place:
Women weep, friends and family cry.

A wake for the victims, tomorrow night is planned,
Pine boxes are made for their rest;
But the job of thawing the bodies, to fit in the boxes:
Challenged Sam Todd's psyche to a test.

The frozen bodies are placed in a warm room to thaw,
Sam Todd keeps the stove stoked hot and red;
But when the thawing bodies began to move and moan;
Sam thought himself the avenged victim of the dead.

It is now Thursday morning, Sam Todd is composed,
Each body is tucked neatly to rest;
The resident priest leads the evening's wake service:
As the sun sets in golden skies of the west.

Friday Morning:

The four bodies are moved to the Mount Carmel Church,
To a common funeral that honors their resign;
They're laid to rest in the cemetery now famous because:
"Of Legends in Frozen Time."

But this is not where the story ends.

The families returned to Hillsdale,
Some move on, yet others stay,
They plant, They harvest, They wed, and give life;
Building tomorrows, as they build their today.

They built roads that led us to highways,
That crossed railroads and interstates on their way.
They built runways and airports; cars, trucks, and sea ports,
They built America and they Flagged Her Their Way.

They went to battle to defend that Flag.
They made America, America today.

Fly your Flag proudly,
Cowboy Poet,
Ray Meyers

OLD GUYS HAVING FUN

Faces that say
what words can't express . . .

CODGERS AND COOTS

Codgers with big hats,
And old horse riding coots;
Share one strong desire"
To die living in their boots.

Dying in the saddle,
Is a cowboy's true desire;
Cowboys don't quit working,
They're too busy to retire.

They take life as it comes,
Their pickup is a dent;
They're usually one month late:
Paying last month's, month late rent.

Codgers with big hats,
And old horse riding coots;
Share one strong desire:
To die living in their boots.

Their heart is ever faithful,
Their soul's honest and true;
Devotedly they tell their woman:
Hon! No one's like you!

Saturday night you will find them,
With their sweet heart at the dance;
Two-stepping from Rap to Polka:
Still in a whirl of first romance.

Codgers with big hats,
Ad old horse riding coots;
Share one strong desire:
To die living in their boots.

Residing in a nursing home,
Would be a cowboy's curse;
Pick a number and wait to die:
How could things get much worse?

But now doctors rebuild cowboys,
With plastic joints and borrowed hearts;
So do we call them used cowboys?
Or just "Recycled Farts?"

Codgers with big hats,
And old horse riding coots;
Share one strong desire:
To die living in their boots.

Watch that rider behind
the rider in front of you!

Cowboy Poet,
Ray Meyers

52

A Lotta Hay

This story took place in the dry plateaus west.
The ranch was called, "Camel—Lot."
The boys called the boss,—Well—We'll just call him Jake:
So now you know the plot.

The boys at the ranch baled hay all week,
Guess, they baled four thousand or more.
The bunkhouse reeked of beer and Ben Gay,
Cowboy's groaned from muscles sore.

Saturday eve Jake stopped by the bunkhouse,
He announced, "Boys I'm weekending in town."
"I thought you all would like to come along?"
But their response was an imminent frown.

"See boys supplies are running kinda short,
And we're plumb out of baler twine."
The boys all knew Jake was sweet on Miss Kate:
And tonight they would dance and dine.

His Wild Country tires spewed clouds of dust, as they ate up the
road to town.
The supply list lay on the dashboard, as Jake and Miss Kate took
to dance,
You see tonight was the special celebration of:
Their thirty-some year romance.

Now Miss Kate was a pretty lady,
She was a sweetheart sort of snot;
But the man she loved was always busy:
So they just never tied the knot.

Monday morning back at the ranch,
The truck loaded full of supplies;
Jake announced he'd met the Indian Chief:
In whose forecasts he trusts and relies.

"Now, boys, The Indian Chief said to me." "This coming
winter's bad."
"There will be freezing rain with heavy snows,"
"Cows will shiver in bighting cold."
"So boys we're baling the hay we can, almost faster than it
grows."

Again Saturday evening rolled around,
Jake was headed to town for supplies;
Now the boys all said, "Jake, just Marry Miss Kate."
"We can see through your alibis."

Jake stomped off, got into his truck,
He thought, "Marrying Miss Kate would be fine;
But I'm so darned busy just running the ranch,
And we're Plum out of baler twine. "

Monday morning Jake returned to the ranch,
With the truck full of baler twine.
He said, "Boys, I've thought about marrying Miss Kate,"
"But let's not rush to change things that are fine."

Oh, By the way, I talked to the Chief.
Winters worse than he imagined so.
For many Moons the wind will rage,
We'll have sleet and heaps of snow.

The boys had been baling hay all week. Again Saturday rolled around.
Cowboy Pete suggested, "Jake, take Miss Kate to the Yuma Herd Bull Show."
"I'll go to town to get supplies; I'll meet with the Indian Chief."
"See Jake, you said, "We need a new bull, "and Miss Kate would love to go! "

So Jake and Miss Kate went to Yuma,
Cowboy Pete went to town for supplies;
But as Pete spoke to the Indian Chief:
He got a, "Real Surprise!"

Pete said, " Old Chief for many years, I've admired your native way,"
" You read the signs of Mother Earth and know just what they say;"
"You say this coming winter's bad. But how can you tell today?"
The Old Chief replied, with a twinkle in his eye. "Ranchers put up a lotta hay."

Keep your rope coiled,
Cowboy Poet,
Ray Meyers

C. P. Zazon

I had a really good cow horse,
His name was C. P. Zazon;
Seems every cowboy I've ever known:
Has had his favorite one.

Granted his name was an awkward one,
Which left me one resort;
To find him another handle:
I called him "Pete" for short.

Pete was not a big horse,
He had registered Arabian Pride;
He had the smoothest walking trot:
In him, I trusted and relied.

I fed him many carrots,
Took pride in his riding gear;
At the end of day when the job was done:
I shared with him my beer.

I kept Pete in a box stall,
To protect him from imminent danger;
But a rabid skunk attacked him there:
He died later by his manger.

Last night a Flu Bug bit me,
My body was achy and sore.
I lay in bed, chilled with a fever,
Of a hundred three or more.

Half dozing I had a vision,
Seems it lasted most the night.
And I saw Old C. P. Zazon;
Coming toward me from The Light.

On a big, white steed running with him,
Was Angel Gabriel all alight;
Pete's steel gray coat after all this time:
Had turned to holy white.

Pete ran right up to me,
I hugged his neck and gave a pat;
With a boost from Good Old Gabriel:
In Pete's saddle I was sat.

Then we took off riding,
We rode for hours that night;
The trail we rode was straight and narrow:
It headed for The Light.

Then Gabriel grabbed on to Old Pete's reins,
He pulled us to a stop;
"Pete missed you, we could hold him no more:
In verdant pastures on the top."

"Well, cowboy you go no further,
Your work is yet undone;
There are calves save and fences to mend:
It's back to work for you now, son."

"So cowboy here's where you get off,
I'm just out here gatherin up strays;
But don't worry cowboy, Pete will be back:
To bring you home in later days."

Happy Trails,
Cowboy Poet,
Ray Meyers

TOBY'S DEBUT

Toby had many spent days practicing,
The coveted two horn rope.
Though he overthrew the rope many times,
Still somehow, Toby knew he had hope.

Now Toby was ready for the arena!
His saddle cinched on a big bay horse.
He challenged himself with a Longhorn cow,
The inevitable test of his pass fail course.

On the far end of the arena,
Cow and horse st-r-a-i-n-ed, at the starting gate!
Hot adrenaline boiling in their blood!
Hey! Steady boy! Now just wait!

With nerves and tensions, like springs of steel.
They burst forth through the starting line!
"Hey! Steady boy, now let's get in sync.
That's it now, were doing just fine!"

Then in sync from off of his dally thumb,
Toby threw the perfect loop!
It looked so pretty sailing through the air,
With the swirl of a Hula-hoop!

The rope dropped over the left horn,
As it looped the right horn first!
It tightened around the cow's horns and poll,
As she lunged in a frenzied burst!

The crowd responded in thunderous applause,
When the announcer recognized Toby's name.
Toby had not only passed his test:
But was entered in Cowboy Hall of Fame!

Suddenly, within an instant!
All action ended; with a snap!
Toby heard chanting to a deep, booming sound.
His radio alarm had been tuned to Rap!

Keep your rope coiled,
Cowboy Poet,
Ray Meyers

BELLE

So much more than a friend.
Born May ninth of thirty eight.
She taught me love with trust and patience:
In years she led me by eight.

Orphaned at birth,
On a warm mid-May morn,
She was loved, often spoiled;
From the time she was born.

Her hair ebony as onyx,
Glowed in sunlight like silk,
Though she never knew the taste;
Of her dear mother's sweet milk.

But what would they name her?
A French man called her, "Belle."
A fitting name for such beauty;
Anybody could tell.

Her eyes true and honest,
Were a deep chestnut brown,
Her skin so black and tender;
Her hair soft as goose down.

She was smart as a whip,
Never attended a school,
But to always serve mankind;
This was her golden rule.

I was a lad just thirteen,
When we shared that first day,
I learned much from this lady;
In a field of lush clover hay.

We shared good times together,
Though she was older than I;
We tread a sea of green corn fields:
Under the warm mid-June sky.

Often we would walk,
She would nuzzle my arm,
At times I'd just hug her;
And reflect on her charm.

Her dark lustrous hair,
How it shown in the sun.
Her legs long and shapely,
She was a beautiful one.

Often while strolling,
Belle would look to the sky;
Fascinated by airplanes:
She would watch as they'd fly.

Ten A.M. every day,
Passed the Sioux City Sue,
A mail plane with twin engines;
And how quickly it flew.

One day seeding oats,
An April shower left us wet;
When we heard this new airplane:
I said they call it a jet.

But Belle liked old airplanes,
Even though jets were new;
See Belle disliked changes:
She would always make do.

Ah! But Sundays free from toil,
Belle lay naked in the sun;
Whisped by waves of Bluegrass:
Belle and nature were one.

Our shared summer was soon over,
As the nights turned off cool.
The summer days we spent together;
Were now my daydreams in school.

And then there were times,
Belle thought were so neat,
Like when I'd trim her toe nails;
Or gently soak her sore feet.

Now Belle was my best mentor,
See she cut me no slack;
She taught me always tug forward:
Don't ever turn back.

All too soon we were parted,
This black beauty and I,
See Belle's doctor told us;
Belle was going to die.

Gone are times we spent together,
Time passes quickly by;
Remember: "Tempus Fugit:"
Or how time does fly.

But there's more to this story,
Than you'd suspicion of course;
You see Belle, this black beauty:
Was my favorite Percheron horse.

Cowboy Poet,
Ray Meyers

Tempus Fugit, BELLE.

COWBOY POETS

How are cowboy poets made?
They don't suddenly just appear,
Now I can't speak for all the rest;
But this is what happened here.

My teachers name was Isaia,
This old sister really had wit,
Her off- time hobby was yodeling;
She taught me poetry in Sophomore Lit.

Soon I'd chosen a favorite poet,
Now he wrote in the sixteenth century,
His words were an intrigue with thoughtful depth;
As he told us of early gentry.

The robes he wore would seem strange to us,
He was no cowboy so don't fear;
He wrote poems of kingdoms and romance;
His "Nom-de-plum" was William Shakespeare.

Years progressed and I gained experience,
From the laughter and tragedy of life;
"You should write a book with all your stories."
Was the suggestion of my wife.

I consistently read in the Cattle Country News,
The stories by Mad Jack Hanks,
He wrote stories and poems, He did cartoons too.
Mad Jack I extend you my thanks.

I was inspired while reading Cowboy Poetry,
That was authored by T. L. Bush.
So I put my stories to rhythm and rhyme:
My leap of faith was really a push.

But the poet whom I most respected,
Whose words flowed and never went slack;
And he wrote many stories of cowboy ways:
He's the poet called Baxter Black.

That pretty well tells the story of how,
A cowboy poet grew midst Iowa corn;
He went from reading to writing in rhythm and rhyme:
And that's how this poet was born.

Keep your rope coiled,
Cowboy Poet,
Ray Meyers

First Day Calving

Well, calving season started today,
The winter has been so mild;
With springtime babies everywhere:
North winds have just gone wild.

This morning the weatherman announced with pride,
"It could snow one inch or flurry;"
I thought, "Not a bad day to start with calving:
Then this storm unleashed all its fury."

The first born was from Bessie,
She had a nice roan bull;
The next one was that little black heifer:
With that breach that we had to pull.

Next is the task of bringing home calves,
That were born out in the storm;
For this I use my trusty hoss Pete:
Sleet stings our face like a swarm.

That big white cow calved in the storm,
She found shelter behind a tree;
"My trusty hoss Pete got skittish and run off:
So baby calf, it's you and me."

Now we're moving, White Mama,
Lead your baby through this snow;
I'm tired and a warm barn waits for you:
We ain't got much farther to go.

I nudge the calf home sideways,
Our progress is steady but slow;
Then I carry the calf behind my neck:
Through that predicted inch of now knee-deep snow.

Back at the barn this baby finds warmth,
There's my faithful hoss Old Pete;
We ride out again to fetch another calf:
From the west field of winter wheat.

Old one-eyed Hereford has a calf out here,
Her right horn points, "Northeast;"
Over there he is huddled in that ravine:
Wow look! He's quite a beast!

With the calf tied in the saddle,
Of my faithful hoss Old Pete;
Hey! Look this cow has got twin calves:
And Pete's running home, How Sweet!

"Well calf, Old Pete got skittish and run off,
With your mama in hot pursuit;
Baby calf, it's you and me treading snow;
Hey! You know, you're kinda cute!"

I'm covered with afterbirth, blood, and mud,
Carrying this calf through white snow on green wheat;
My waterproof Carharts are heavy and wet:
Numb toes sting the end of my feet.

Back at the barn Pete's dancing around,
As that Hereford lets out a snort;
I remove the calf from Pete's saddle:
To discover my rein's just got short.

In the barn everyone's back together now,
As the storm continues to rage;
I enter each calf in my pocket herd book:
Today's calves nearly fill the page.

Then I feed my faithful Hoss Old Pete,
He helped me—Well—part of the day;
So why do I call him Faithful Pete?
Well—he's—faithful—at running away.

I search to find some clean dry clothes,
It's the third time I've changed today;
Now I look like I've shopped at a rummage sale:
Or that, scare—a—crow, stuffed with hay.

With the tractor I help get the school bus unstuck,
Then help a baby calf find its first nurse;
Then it's feeding and bedding the yearlings:
By dark the storm's fury grows worse.

I'm back in the ranch house. My dear wife says,
"Supper's about ready so just watch the news;"
On the floor by the TV, It's so comfy and warm:
Good idea, I'll just—watch—the—n e w z z z z z z .

Keep those O B chains handy,
Cowboy Poet,
Ray Meyers

I Wonder if I'm a Cowboy

I was wondering as I checked my cows,
Who really is a cowboy today?
And then I pondered this question:
Am I one? And who's to say?

I don't sleep on a saddle in under the stars,
I don't ride the trail for months on end;
I don't eat beans by a rustic chuck wagon:
But I live on a ranch, round the bend.

I don't drive to rodeos in a fancy truck,
To team rope, I always miss heals;
T he truck I drive is full of dents:
Heck, it's lucky it still has wheels.

I don't ride saddle broncs at the rodeo,
But I've been bucked off once or twice;
I've never roped calves at a rodeo:
But I've roped cows and poured 'em for lice.

I've never dogged steers at a rodeo,
But I've dogged bulls and made 'em steers;
I've never rode bulls or bare back broncs:
Those that do I've respected for years.

71

At the National Anthem I face Old Glory,
And reflect how I served her with pride;
While I'm reminiscent of our MIA's:
And friends who while serving her died.

I don't wear cowboy boots when I do my work,
It's lace boots with arch supports;
But I wear cowboy boots when I go to town:
Go to church or play contact sports.

I don't wear clothes with billboard signs,
Like Justin, P.B.R., Coors, or Bud;
My jacket is tattered, my shirt is torn:
My jeans are stained with cows' blood.

I don't jump around and holler Garth songs,
Or play a guitar on a bar stool;
But Sundays I sing at the church in the choir:
And attend all the plays down at school.

I don't wear silk shirts with ruffles and stuff,
I've never ridden on a tin bull;
I don't wear my hat all stuck full of pins:
But sweat stains my hat's crown to the full.

I don't know the names of the latest country songs,
I don't party and drink until two;
I don't do line dance at a big city bar:
But Mam' I will two-step with you.

I don't ride through town for Easter Seals,
River City Roundup and all those affairs;
'Cause I'm busy tendin to the needs of my cows:
Sayin we need rain Lord, Oh please hear our prayer.

I was wonderin as I checked my cows,
Who really is a cowboy today?
And then I pondered this question:
Am I one? And who's to say?

And then the answer came to me,
Does it matter what people say?
I've got family, a ranch; cows, dog, horses, and friends:
And I'm livin a full life in my way!

Keep your rope coiled,
Cowboy Poet,
Ray Meyers

MUZZIE

Travis was the best cow dog—
On this ranch—well—or was he?
Maybe until I came along,
I'm a border collie called "The Muzzie."

I was made at home on this ranch,
My new Master had been hurt:
But I showed him fun and gave him joy:
I was always so alert!

I love to work and play fun games,
My favorite "Fetch the Glove."
No matter how far you'd throw it,
I'd bring it back with love

My long coat had a bounce,
My color black and white
And when I didn't understand:
I'd tilt my head to the right.

With baby calves I'd often play,
I'd lick their ears and sniff their nose;
But those old bulls on the other hand:
Gave the impression, "Don't impose!"

Working cattle came so natural,
Its merits I could savor;
Working gave me more reward:
Than any doggie biscuit's flavor.

I'd bring the cattle home,
Like a train on the rail;
Or like a neat bound package:
That's delivered in your mail.

I'd bark at their nose,
I'd hang on their tail;
I'd nip at their heels:
I'd take em on down the trail.

I'd flank to the left!
I'd flank em to the right!
I'd heel them up the middle:
With just a nippy bite.

Baby calves were fun to work,
For at them I'd gently pounce;
And off they'd run to Mama:
In a gate of gallopy bounce!

My family was all gathered,
And ball with them I played;
When suddenly! "There's a rabbit!"
It's so much fun on Saturday!

Life had so much fun!
That fun itself would interrupt;
So much of life I had to live:
When shocking death came so abrupt.

I'm buried in green pastures,
With the cows that I drove;
There's a pond with restful waters:
Just down the hill below that grove,

He says that dogs don't have a soul,
But listen Reverend, Let's clear it;
Have you never—ever heard:
That doggies just have spirit.

Heaven is man's soul,
With their Master up above;
Dog's heaven is our spirit:
In our Master's heart with love.

So pull yourself together,
Weeping makes life look fuzzy;
And get on with your life:
With the Spirit of The Muzzie!

Cowboy Poet,
Ray Meyers

Muzzie, a victim of animal abuse, was senselessly killed by repeated shotgun blasts in front of his 11- year- old master, who was right there to retrieve his dog.

Muzzie's crime: He followed that rabbit to a brush pile on a neighbor's property.

Muzzie died in the arms of his master as he was carried home.

SALUTE

From the coliseum of Rome's great Empire.
To liberty's home on this date;
There are scrolls of war's great heroes:
But it was his spirit that made this one great.

He's not buried among Arlington's Heroes,
There is no monument to honor his grave;
Just a simple rock marker in Old Fort Sill:
His reward for the life that he gave.

Most Americans don't know his biography,
History labeled him a ruthless killer;
And if Hollywood ever made a movie of his life:
It'd be a cliff-hanging silver screen thriller.

His ancestors faced extermination attempts,
Of Spanish Conquistadors for three hundred years;
His people who were reduced to raiding for food:
Developed their sense of keen nose, eyes, and ears.

He was born into a world with a price on his head,
It is said, "He was a son of his day;"
He was a member of the Chiricahua Apache:
His name was Goyathlay.

Settlers in droves took Apache land,
In what is today Arizona—New Mexico;
They exploited the land of treasure and wealth:
Leaving the Apache with no place to go.

Goyathlay, who was a medicine man,
Returned from trading with a neighboring village;
To find that summer day of Eighteen Fifty Eight:
Mexican Soldiers turned him victim of pillage.

His aged Mother, young Wife, and three children,
Were all among the slain;
Now Goyathlay, The Medicine Man:
Was turned warrior from his pain.

He declared war on exploiting settlers,
Both Mexican and American alike;
He went on to raid white soldiers' camps:
To survive he had to strike.

His raids were sensationalized by the press,
They labeled him, "Savage Killer;"
But the massacre of Apache women and children:
Was left out for paid ads and filler.

In search of freedom he defeated armies,
When outnumbered a hundred to one;
He defied death and fought for thirty-some years:
"Of His Time He Was A Son."

Congress pressured to eliminate Apaches,
And many wars were fought;
Until when betrayed by Apache Army Scouts;
The Army imprisoned the Warrior they sought.

Goyathlay, and his new family,
Were held in Florida as prisoners of war;
They were marched to Mt. Vernon, Alabama:
Then Fort Sill to be free never more.

He never was an Apache Chief,
A mistaken press falsely named him so;
He was a medicine man who wielded spiritual powers:
The world knows him as Geronimo.

Geronimo died of pneumonia,
Falling from his horse one wintry night;
On February Seventeenth, Nineteen Hundred Nine:
His freed spirit had won its fight.

This story is not a happy one,
It's quite sad as stories go;
How this man sought for freedom in the, "Land of the Free:
From his spirit may freedom flow.

Rest in Peace,
Cowboy Poet,
Ray Meyers

80

THE AMERICAN WINDMILL

Born ahead of their time,
Windmills predated ecology;
When pumping water with wind:
Was just a dream of technology.

Man's harness on the wind,
Born of industrial revolution;
Turned gears of the twentieth century:
To water pumping revolution.

They pumped water from a well,
Into a cistern or a tank;
Found on deep paths to the barn:
Where tired horses bowed and drank.

Windmills dotted the prairie,
Every farm it seems had one;
Serving cool, refreshing water:
When a hard day's work was done.

With tails astern that pierced the wind,
When the winds changed they would drone;
Moaning brakes in eerie—gusty—dark night.
Shivered spines of those home alone.

On a wheel with its sails spinning free unfurled.
A wheel in the wind's embrace;
Sometimes rocking just half turns:
To the wind's uncertain pace,

The legs were tripod, most had four,
Or wooden towers ten feet high;
Some reached to eighty feet high, some more:
Catching winds up in the sky.

Their ladders were a thrill of adventure,
When wobbly weak rungs would break;
Or the pump rod would set to motion:
And the tower would nudge and then quake.

There was Aermotor, Chicago, and Butler,
Fairbury, Dempster, and Star;
Sears—Kenwood and Montgomery Ward:
But Eurica was cheaper by far.

There was Sandwich, Wheeler, and Haladay,
Eclipse had sails of wood;
Pumping water for railroads and cattle:
Devoted to duty they stood.

Eurica boasted an economy kit,
You assembled it yourself;
Butler competed with zinc coated steel:
Ball bearings gave it stealth.

Then Sears came out with Kenwood;
The affordable steel machine;
Montgomery Ward's answer, a twenty dollar steel kit:
That you assembled to keep the price lean.

Aermotor's steel was galvanized,
It had cups to oil the machine;
Fairbury and Dempster closed in nineteen sixty,
And ended their wind-blown dream.

With a whiskey bottle of oil in hand,
We oiled windmills in younger days;
Cowboys climbing windmill towers found:
Height advantage for finding strays.

Yet it's hard feeling romantic about windmills,
Fixing em on a cold winter's day;
With your fingers froze tight to a tower of ice, from cold:
Or f-r-i-g-h-t maybe would you say?

Check your curb strap lately?
Cowboy Poet
Ray Meyers

But like unto a Spielberg Movie.
When you thought The American Windmill was dead,
It's reborn to create electricity:
With a tall sleek three bladed head!

THE OLD ROCKFORD WATCH

"I really wonder what time it is,"
Said the foreman of the corn shelling crew;
The old cowman pulled a silver watch from his bibs:
It was the size of a can of chew.

"I just set my watch on Saturday, so it could be a little slow,"
"It's twenty-five after, on second thought, better make that half
past two;"
"WOW! That's quite an old watch," The foreman said;
"Bet it could tell a story or two."

Said the cowman. "It's a Rockford, I've carried it sixty-five
years,"
"And yes, it could tell a few."
"To set it you screw loose the crystal ring,"
"Then remove the crystal from its seat;"

"Then pull the stem—just—half—way—up."
"My Grandson once said this was neat."
"Then set the hands with your pocket knife,"
"Assemble it and it should—beat—."

"It was a gift from my Dad," The cowman said,
As he listened to its twelve / eights tic-ñtic sound.
"My Dad bought it new from a jeweler in town,"
"About eight years he carried it around."

84

"I crushed the case a few years back, when my chest hit the
saddle horn."
"I jumped a ditch on a horse called Mac, man could he cover
ground."
"I pulled the pieces from my pocket—one—by—one,"
"And took them to the jewelry store;"

The jeweler took the pieces, shook his head,
Then said. "Bet your chest is sore."
"But he put all the pieces in a brand new case,"
"And it ran about twelve years more."

"Then over the years the metal wore thin,"
"And somehow I dented the case."
"The Roman Numerals were faded—I could read them no
more;"
"So we just gave it a whole new face."

"The stem was replaced at least two or three times,"
And the Cowman listened—to its time—ticking—pace.
It was that same secure tic that once lulled his daughter to sleep,
When after dinner she sat on his lap;

"Don't dwop it, don't fling it, don't bing it," She'd say:
And drift off into peaceful nap.
Then with huge callused hands, he laid her gently in bed:
And tucked her in with a warm loving wrap.

Mid-morning one day, it's ticking sound stopped,
Never, ever to tick again.
Now it rests in a glass case as a reminder of:
The Cowman and his stories of back when.

Tempus fugit
Cowboy Poet
Ray Meyers

A COWBOY'S VIRGIN PRAIRIE

From the confusions of adolescence,
In her succor I would hide:
Where through wafts of vegetative fragrance:
And avon symphonies I ride.

I hear soft, lazy gurgles,
As pristine waters their level seek;
A froggy voice strongly leads a chorus:
Of amphibian unison to praise the creek.

A homebound muskrat swims up stream,
Then dives to his burrow below a log;
The froggy chorus is abruptly silenced:
By the rippling k-pluke of a diving frog.

Mosquitoes sing falsetto, in a concert of soprano humming,
Distinguishingly, they daintily dance, forming tiny clouded poufs;
I'm mesmerized by the steady rhythmic clopping:
Beats of my equine's walking hoofs.

Then quietly tall grasses rustle,
As a doe escapes in cautious fear;
Of the ballet beauties on the virgin prairie:
None compare to the grace of a flighting deer.

Near the edge of the prairie's meadow.
Where the elevations raise;
The awe of hills in twilight's shadows:
Rise in homage to their prairie's praise.

We contour and climb to the prairie's ridge,
Just man, his horse, and the creak of leather;
With labored horses breath and pungent equine lather:
Man and horse crest the ridge together.

A-top the virgin prairie, grow grasses lush and tall,
Where from below earth touched the sky;
Now horizons elude into distant walls:
And paint a panorama, to captivate the eye.

Her soils run deep, full of richness and life,
Amid fields sick from chemicals of greed;
Their soils eroded from plows and tillage:
Gave their life to sustain human need.

Treasured as our own soul's food,
Born to us of the Virgin Mary;
So treasured to cows, are the nurturing grasses:
Born to them of the virgin prairie.

I've drawn from her strength, in times of trouble,
I've traveled her trails for fifty some years;
Reminiscent of urban cliff dwellers, stoned high:
Wondering how do they conquer their fears?

As sun pales into the dusk of night,
I'm immersed in a globe of stars;
I become a part of the Milky Way:
Big Dipper, Mercury, Venus, and Mars.

I hear the song of the coyote's howl,
A night hawk swiftly swoops by;
As I mount my horse for the ride back home:
A jet pulls its trail through the sky.

This prairie once covered all of Iowa,
She's now an oasis in a desert of corn;
For this lady died raped and ravaged for profit:
So few know her, there's no one to mourn.

This virgin prairie is such a beauteous land,
To think her scope was as huge as thunder;
Now it's rare to find what once covered the earth:
What have we done? I'm left to wonder.

Check your curb strap lately?
Cowboy Poet,
Ray Meyers

THE COWBOY TEST

"I want to be a cowboy, Dad,
So tell me where I begin;"
"I can ride a horse, I can swing a rope:
I rode a bull even though he did win."

"My Son, My son, The dad begun,
I'm proud of you, you're better than best;"
"But if you want to be a cowboy son:
You must pass this lifelong test."

"You see it starts out easy Son,
Checkin cows in early May;"
"And the month old calves all look so pretty:
Eating grass on a warm spring day."

"But then the month of June comes by,
You're hot and dirty from baling hay;"
"The flies start biting and the calves get Pink Eye:
They all looked so pretty last May."

"In July's hot sun combining needs done,
You itch from oats, bearded barley, and wheat;"
"Some of the calves picked up pneumonia:
But next winter they'll need grain to eat."

"Then August comes, it's supposed to be dry,
But you get hit with a twelve inch rain;"
"And some of those calves, and your water gaps:
Well, they all just went down the drain."

"September rolls around and this month is famous,
For Durns—Disappointments—and, Oh—No's!"
"Cause you been so busy taking care of the herd:
That you missed all the rodeos."

"In October you find yourself harvesting corn,
The combine stops with a clatter;"
"The cylinder is sprung, the concaves are bent:
By that rock that didn't shatter."

"Now it's November, It's time to wean calves,
Last year's heavies are in the feedlot unsold;"
"The corn isn't combined; you're grease to your elbows:
And the weather is turning cold."

"December comes by, You're caught up on your work,
Then you notice your horse by the gate."
"Month by month you've ignored him, He wanted to work:
But all he could do was wait."

Durn!

Cowboy Poet
Ray Meyers

THE FISCAL CALENDAR'S CLOSE

The Cowboy's Christmas comes twice a year,
It happens first in the very late fall;
Cold, crisp air resounds with the seasonal song of:
Cattle caroling their Post Weaning Bawl

The cowboy's Christmas tree is his weaning pen,
Each ornament is a big healthy calf;
Each one crafted and nourished by the cowboy's love:
He reminisces those tough times with a laugh.

Like Santa Claus, the Cowboy's Lord is good,
Each bawling gift gives the cowboy delight;
And falling asleep, He dabs a tear of joy:
The weaning song lullabies him tonight.

The crescendoing song fills the frosty night,
By second day, it's a deafening roar;
The harmonizing of cattle in Moo's and Maa's:
Fills chilled air with a swelling soar.

The song filters through dawn's golden Aspen leaves,
Through Red Maples, Tall Pines, Spruce, and Fir;
And it fills the cowboy's heart with joy:
It's been a good year the cowboy is sure.

The music of weaning decrescendos and subsides
With the third weaning day's setting sun;
There'll be immunizing and pouring, ear tagging, and more:
This Cowboy's New Year has just begun.

Merry Christmas,
Cowboy Poet
Ray Meyers

A City Christmas Tree

The cowboy pondered, then asked himself.
"How many winters had he spent with this herd?"
He reminisced as he recounted.
"This would be his forty- third."

Now a line shack can get mighty lonely,
When it's just you that's tending the cows;
In the cradle of a high mountain's valley:
Remote from paved roads and snow plows.

He wasn't just sure what day it was.
But it surely was now mid-December;
The time for his ritual Christmas tree hunt:
Like he'd done long as he could remember.

There's just something about your horse dragging home,
A Fir—A Spruce—or a Pine;
Last year he found one nearly three miles up:
Beneath a shelf on the timberline.

But this year the cowboy thought differently,
He'd pick a day and just break free;
In the mild weather, He'd take his pickup truck:
And buy a city tree.

His day for tree shopping had now arrived,
He drove down the mountain; It was cool but fair;
But 30 miles below at the edge of town:
There were flurries in the air.

The cowboy found a plastic Christmas tree,
At the big city's shopping mart;
Then he read the assembly directions:
As he placed it in his cart.

Insert branches A into slots B through K,
Then open needles to form a tree;
Then insert the tree into its base:
The cowboy thought. It's just not me.

He walked up the street to a Christmas tree sale,
Just across from the courthouse square;
And a fresh forest scent drifted by on a breeze:
From this store in the open air.

A sign at the gate read four dollars a foot,
Sizes five-foot, six, eight, and ten;
And the evergreen scent made the cowboy think:
He was back atop his mountain again.

There were trees decorated in garland and light,
Some were sprayed to make them look snowy white;
They were full and flocked and trimmed in symmetry:
Then he saw one, its shape was just right.

It was ten feet tall, with some branches gone,
With longer branches on its shaded north side;
The bark was skinned and the trunk was bowed:
It looked as natural as an eight-second ride.

With the ten-foot tree loaded in his eight- foot truck bed,
He would haul it with an open tail gate;
He started his truck and was ready to leave:
When intuition told him to wait.

Then her sobbing story caught his attention,
He couldn't leave just yet;
He listened as she told her story of ill fate:
It was tough as misfortunes can get.

Her son was in need of special lenses,
With her story she did proceed
"In a year he would be completely blind:"
And the story unfolded her need.

This would be the very last Christmas,
That her son could see a tree:
She wanted for her son this special Christmas gift:
Hers was certainly an unselfish plea.

The Doctor bills for her son were voracious,
They ate deeply into her purse;
Now she had no money for a Christmas tree:
And needs at home made their matters much worse.

Her story continued till the cowboy said,
"I've heard enough lady, Please just stop;"
He grabbed a saw and from his Christmas tree:
Cut six feet from the very top.

He tied the tree to the roof of her car,
With a frayed old lariat rope;
And looking at now what was left of his tree:
He felt good for he had given hope.

The cowboy commenced with his homeward journey,
Hauling his topless four foot of tree;
When he came upon a group of picketers protesting:
The closure of their factory.

Their jobs had gone south at the managers whim,
Cheaper labor, lower taxes, and freight;
The picketers shivered in the freezing cold front:
Would he help them or pass by, Oh, no wait!

The cowboy pulled off to the side of the road,
He cut branches from the back of his tree;
That side could be hidden against the wall;
He wouldn't miss them and nobody would see.

With the branches he started a small warming fire,
Picketers warmed with his gesture of love;
But the fire wouldn't last long, so he swiped from his tree:
Two more feet from the very top of.

Just a mile down the road, He drove by a church,
With a country Nativity Scene;
But something was missing, it looked cold and naked:
It needed the warmth of an evergreen.

So again the cowboy pulled off of the road,
He cut the remaining branches from his tree;
And with a scrap of barbed wire he made a wreath:
He gave God the last of his tree.

Once home the cowboy took the two feet of trunk,
He set it thoughtlessly inside his shacks door;
Then donning his Carharts and warm leather gloves:
Set out to check his cows once more:

He returned to his shack. It was almost dark,
He made a drink of hot cider and brandy;
Then lighting a candle he set it on the tree stump:
Without thought but because it was handy.

Humming a Christmas hymn, He reclined in his rocker,
Glimpsed the candle with its tree trunk host;
He thought:
"It sure doesn't look like much of a tree:
But it's done more good than most."

Merry Christmas!

Keep your rope coiled,
Cowboy Poet,
Ray Meyers

98

OH NOBLE COW

As a species I'm called Bovine,
At the table I'm called Beef;
But this story that I tell you:
Is far beyond belief.

The event was predicted,
In a Testament of Old;
It took place here in my stable:
I was the first one to behold.

They had traveled a great distance,
Their names, Joseph and Mary;
And the beast that Mary rode:
To me looked scruffy, and scary.

They registered in Bethlehem,
As required by Caesar's law;
And God's Word was unfolding:
As old prophets has foresaw.

Now Mary was with child,
Her Babe would free man from sin;
They both looked so cold, so tired:
There was no room at the inn.

They made their home in my stable,
As it came to pass;
By now their Long Eared Jack:
Was really biting my grass!

Well I shared my very best hay,
They all looked so forlorn;
Then later on that evening:
Baby Jesus was born.

Then all Heaven broke loose!
Many angels went winging;
They flitted and they fluttered:
Glad Hosannas they were singing!

Shepherds from the hills,
Came to see The Holy Child;
And they brought along their—smelly sheep:
Couldn't leave them in the wild.

What's happened to my peaceful stable?
Jack's feasting like a glutton!
And now what's worse, with all those—sheep—?!!
My home: Has the stench—of mutton!!

Home was such a peaceful place,
I could lie and sleep all night;
Now! That bright star—shining—overhead.
Instills in me a fright!

People stop, they bring a gift,
A blanket, a lamb, a comb.
What can I give—here where I live?
I'll share with Him my home!

I'll give to Him a pail of milk!
I'll share my body heat.
But, I hope—these—folks—all—move along;
Before they get hungry for meat!

Three kings ride in on camels,
They travel from afar;
They speak of names I've never heard:
Casper—Malchior—Balthasar ? ? ?

People differ in how they talk,
In the language that they choose:
Cows don't low or go Hee Haw!
Cows speak in simple Moos!

The kings bring gifts to The Radiant Child,
Of gold incense and myrrh;
I'm so frightened by those camels that:
My memory's all a blur.

A cow has needs but simple ones,
Some hay, some drink, some grain;
We live our life for the simple things:
Like the smell of a sudden rain.

A cow has needs but simple ones,
A home that's free from mud,
A stable that's dry with lots of hay:
A place to chew our cud.

Joseph and kings are sleeping now,
Angel voices fill their head;
"Vacation Egypt."—"Take the scenic route:"
"Herod wants The Christ Child dead."

Then came the dawn in a distant haze,
I heard a rooster crow;
Soon rose the sun, it shown so bright:
It gave a warming glow.

They packed up Jack, kings mounted their camels,
Mary wore her traveling dress;
And they took to the road at a frantic pace:
All they left here was—emptiness.

So listen my calf and tell the tale,
Of how God saw a cow's true worth;
For he chose a cow's home,—a stable:
For the place of—His—Only—Son's—birth.

Merry Christmas!

Cowboy Poet,
Ray Meyers

GRANDMA'S MINCEMEAT

4 Quarts. Cooked, sweet applesauce
(1/4 inch chunks of apples are ideal.)
3 cups sautéed hamburger.
1 cup broth from sautéed hamburger.
3 cups Raisins 1 cup Brown Sugar
½ t Salt 5 t Cinnamon
3 t Nutmeg 2 ½ t Ginger
2 ½ t Allspice 2 ½ t Cloves

Mix together the above ingredients and
Simmer for one hour, stir often.

Add 2 ½ cups Whiskey or Brandy
And bring to a simmer again.

Pour immediately into sterile pint jars and seal.
Makes about 10 pints.

One pint of mincemeat will make one pie.

Add 1 T minute tapioca to mincemeat before
Pouring it into an unbaked pie shell.

Bake at 350 degrees for 45 minutes,
Or until crust is golden brown.

RAY'S (KICK #%@) BAKED BEANS

5 lbs. Navy Beans 1 t Black Pepper
2 t Garlic Powder 3 T Salt
2 T Baking soda

Cover with 3 inches of water and let soak overnight.
Next morning beans need to be covered with 1 inch of water.

Add
5 Chopped Green Peppers 5 Chopped Onions
2ñ26 oz cans of spaghetti sauce with cheese
1 qt. Bar-B-Que sauce 1 T Liquid Smoke
2 t Basil 2 t Sage
2 cups Vinegar 4 cups Dark Brown Sugar
2 lbs. Chopped, Fried, and Drained Bacon.

Stir ingredients together.

Bake at 350 degrees for 3 hours.
Thicken with corn starch to desired texture.

Makes about 14 Quarts.
Can be packaged and frozen in portions for later use.

Janell's Macaroni Salad

1 lb. Macaroni cooked and drained.
1 green pepper finely chopped 4 carrots finely chopped
1 onion finely chopped 1 cup sugar
1 can sweetened condensed milk ½ cup vinegar
1 cup mayonnaise 1 t salt
¼ t black pepper

Makes about 5 quarts.

Ray's Coffee bread

2 cups whole wheat flour ½ cup white flour
2 t baking soda 1 t salt
2 cups plain yogurt ½ cup sorghum
1 cup raisins or maraschino cherries ¾ cup black walnuts

Sift dry ingredients together.
Combine yogurt, fruit, and sorghum.
Blend the two mixtures together until the flour is evenly moist.
Divide the mixture into two pre-greased bread pans.

Bake at 350 degrees for 45 minutes.
Serve thinly sliced with cream cheese.

BLUE PAINT

At a Veterans' rest home, on the sunny east lawn,
He had been dozing since early dawn;
To a nurse he said, "My grandson's coming to see me."
Then he stretched out his arms with a yawn.

Every Thursday they would spend precious time together,
This old man and his four year grandson;
While the boy's mother did shopping and picked up the
groceries;
Their time was from eleven to one.

Excitedly, the little boy jumped up on Grandpa's lap,
Said, "Tell me a story Grandpa, please."
"I like to hear those stories you tell of:
When you had legs below your knees."

The old man smiled, hugged the child and said,
"I've just the story though its time is quite quaint;
It's the story about a little roping horse:
A little mare and her name was Blue Paint."

"The story took place a long time ago,
Before the war of Two Thousand Three;
And the way the old man told the story:
It was so real you could touch it and see.

Toby was a third year veterinary student,
He read his books, oh he studied hard;
His education was a grant, an enlistment bonus:
From the Iowa National guard.

Toby also loved roping. He spent hours practicing each day,
Looping wind and swinging sisal around.
Or else he'd be roping those plastic steer heads;
Jumping loops or just dallying around.

Toby entered calf roping rodeo events,
He practiced roping everywhere;
And it seemed whenever Toby threw a loop:
He'd seldom miss or come up roping air.

Toby was well liked by his comrade cowboys,
But he had a problem, quite serious of course;
And that was whenever Toby wanted to rope:
He had to borrow a horse.

Now you'd think a cowboy, who had no horse,
Would be the butt of many a jeer.
Except Toby worked hard to get through vet school:
He studied hard and his goal was sincere.

Toby lived alone on a forty-acre ranch,
On the east slope of Leheigh's west side;
The house Toby lived in was beyond repair:
He'd build a new house for his someday new bride.

Just downhill from Toby's ranch,
And in Leheigh downhill's a direction;
Lived a cute little blonde her name was Shari:
She was the heart throb of Toby's affection.

Shari ran a little home cookin' cafe,
On the lower side of Leheigh's main street.
Toby would stop in for the noon day special:
Home made pie and Shari's kiss so discrete.

Toby had it figured that in two more years,
He would finish his veterinary school.
He'd make Shari his bride, but more important now:
This ropin' calves without a horse wasn't cool.

So Toby set out to find him a horse,
That was cheaper than a breeding fee;
Then he saw a news ad, "Horse sale in Story City:"
Could he afford one? He would just have to see.

It was an awfully slow day at the Story City Auction,
Yet the auctioneer's cry did prevail;
And the next lot to sell was a gray mare, All but dead:
With ski hooves, a big head, and no tail.

Upon entering the sale ring the gray mare stumbled,
She wavered, and then fell with a thud.
But the auctioneer praised; She'll foal sometime this year!
She's an opportunity just waiting to bud!

Gimme a hundert dollars - common gimme two,
You know she's worth at least four!
As the auctioning continued;
The mare again stumbled; she wavered, and fell once more.

Boys bid me ten dollars,
Come on now fifteen.
Toby bought her,
Through a bidding gesture unseen.

After everyone had loaded and left the sale,
Toby paid for and loaded the mare;
He squelched the jeering office, when these words he said.
"Her colt's a ropin' horse!" They said, sure, with a stare.

Toby hauled the mare to his Leheigh ranch,
It was a small place overlooking the town;
His old Dodge pickup rumbled while descending Leheigh's hill:
Nearing the bottom Toby again shifted down.

The trailer pushed Toby's pickup past the corner bar and grill,
Then it smoked up the hill out of town;
A parade of his friends beat Toby to his ranch:
Toby greeted his friends with a frown.

Toby unloaded the lame gray mare,
In an orchard across the yard;
Then left to serve his weekend duty:
With the Iowa National Guard.

With his cell phone, while driving to the weekend drill,
Toby dialed up his girlfriend Shari;
He asked her to check on his old gray mare:
He said she wobbles so please do be wary.

November's chill turned to December's snow,
Then in the midst of a January thaw;
The old gray mare gave birth to a filly:
The most pathetic colt you ever saw.

She was tobiano Paint. Her coat was white,
Her spots were as black as could be;
She had spindly crooked legs and a long skinny face"
She was skinny as a singletree.

She worked a long time just to stand and nurse,
And her Ma Ma didn't have much for dinner;
By the time the filly was one week old"
She was taller and a little bit thinner.

The Old Gray Mare grew thinner too,
Her teeth were too long to eat;
Then on one cold morning she lay by her filly:
As her spirit had taken retreat.

Toby took the filly into his house,
He made a pen in the warmth of his cellar
What should he do with such a runty colt?
Well if she lived he would probably just sell her.

Toby fed the filly a diet of powdered milk,
Sometimes three, mostly four times a day;
By now she was starting to gain some weight:
She nibbled grain and munched on hay.

Then one spring day Toby got, "The Call."
He called Shari, said I've a job for you;
Could you feed my colt and sell her some day:
It's the best for her I can do.

I've been called by the Guard. See we're going to war,
There are terrorists and the world is chaotic.
It's my duty as a Guardsman to serve my country;
To be loyal and patriotic.

Both to and from work, Shari stopped by the ranch,
She had fallen in love with the filly;
It never crossed her mind to give the colt a name:
Mostly she just called the colt silly.

The filly got stronger, her legs grew straight,
Things go right when their treated with love;
Toby and Shari wrote letters to each other each day:
A match was being made from above.

Six months passed, the filly's spots changed,
They had shed from black to blue roan;
Her white coat beneath blue roan spots shown so bright:
And my how the young colt had grown.

Toby drove a truck from Camp Arifjan in Kuwait,
He hauled in trucks that stalled out in Iraq;
The days were hard and long and hot was the sun:
Each night Toby welcomed his rack.

But Toby practiced roping nearly every day,
Seems he roped every tank and truck;
Roping helped Toby pass the lonesome time:
His buddies said Toby brought them good luck.

One day in Iraq in the mid of June,
Toby was helping to load a stalled truck;
A winch was winding to load a stalled truck:
When Toby's fate was dealt a blow of bad luck.

Toby directed the loading procedure,
As he stood near the stalled truck's back tire;
The truck rolled ahead off the mine it compressed:
There was a boom and a hot flash of fire.

Toby was lifted and hurled through the air,
He remembered nothing of hitting the ground;
A medic scurried to stop Toby's profuse bleeding:
His scythed off legs were nowhere to be found.

What happened to Toby and the sequence it followed,
Well, Toby really wasn't quite sure;
There was a helicopter ride, a doctor talking to him:
The time was a confusing blur.

A familiar voice then called his name,
There was the warmth of someone holding his hand;
Then Toby awakened to see Shari's sweet smile:
She said I love you Toby, I'm here with you, and. . . .

Again Toby drifted into peaceful sleep,
But now everything was ok;
Just knowing that Shari was by his side:
Made everything right, in its way.

Two days later Toby awakened again,
There was Shari still by his side;
He said I love you Shari, I want us to marry:
Oh Shari would you please be my bride.

Shari was quite taken by Toby's request,
But in an instant she said. Yes! I will!
Toby didn't know yet that his legs were gone;
Then a nurse came to him with a pill.

Let's see how those bandages are doing now,
The nurse threw back the sheet with a flair;
But when Toby saw that his legs were gone:
He just looked into space with a stare.

For the next two days Toby did not speak,
Without legs, what could life have in store?
But Shari stayed with Toby, she held his hand:
She said we will marry as we planned before.

The doctors tried in vain to cheer Toby up,
Seems Toby had given up hope;
But Shari knew Toby, and she got him to smile:
When she gave him that lariat rope.

Toby practiced his dallies, and working his rope,
He perfected his inside loop;
He roped a few nurses and showed off for them:
While his rope danced the hula-hoop.

Shari told Toby her many stories,
About his horse Little Blue Paint;
How now she had grown to thirteen hands:
But Toby argued. She's a scrub! And she ain't!

Those next few weeks how quickly they passed,
With surgeries and therapy of sorts;
Then Shari presented Toby with a gift:
Of Levis cut off into shorts.

Yet Toby practiced roping every day,
Seems every nurse had fallen victim to his rope;
Toby roped everything, be it moving or still:
The lariat had given Toby new hope.

Doctors tried fitting Toby with prosthetic legs,
They looked pretty in a suit and dress shoe;
But Toby wanted legs that did more than look good;
Doc said sorry. That's the best I can do.

Toby was discharged and sent to his home,
Where his demeanor grew more ugly each day;
Until one day in an ugly exchange of verbiage:
Toby chased his love Shari away.

Bitter by the confines of life in a wheel chair,
The false legs Toby refused to wear;
Toby wished for just legs on which he could walk:
But his life just seemed doomed to this chair.

Bitter and angry, Toby spent his days alone,
His life's goal was to have one more drink;
But his sorrows would not drown, his fears would not leave:
Till at last he could not even think.

Shari spent her days working in that small café,
Blue Paint now consumed her free time:
They did poles and barrels and all kind of games:
They had a oneness of rhythm and rhyme.

Toby hit bottom for about three weeks or four,
He hated people, He chased off his friends;
Till a social worker from The Veterans' Affairs:
Convinced Toby this is not where life ends.

Toby was taken to the Veterans' Hospital,
Where they helped him to overcome booze;
They helped Toby decide what kind of life he would live:
And how to live the sort of life he would choose.

Toby was confused as to who he was,
And why did this fate come to him?
Then he met this Rabbi who had no arms:
Together they exercised in the gym.

The Rabbi explained the Old Book says,
We are made in the image of God;
So if we want to know. Just who we are?
We first must learn about God.

God said to Moses my name is I Am,
I Am here before time began;
I Am good, I Am justice, I Am power, and all:
To know yourself you must know who I Am.

Toby thanked the Rabbi, They became good friends,
He never forgot what that Rabbi had taught;
So Toby gave up drinking, He was an image of God:
To learn of God is now what Toby sought.

Life changed for Toby, Things were suddenly sure,
Baptized in the confidence of his God who is near;
He thought of his life. The things he'd done in fear:
Then wrote to Shari; He said I need you, my dear.

Shari and Blue paint rode by Toby's ranch each day,
Let's stop today Blue Paint, What you say?
Toby's treasured new rope lay-a-tangle in tall grass:
With teary eyes Shari rode quietly away.

Riding back to her driveway, Shari talked to Blue Paint,
How she missed Toby, as she picked up the mail;
There was a letter from Toby—Shari opened it and read:
Then like Blue lightning they sped up the trail.

Shari threw off the saddle, put Blue Paint in her yard,
"I got a letter from Toby!" She said.
She tossed the mare a bale of hay:
Then off to Toby she sped.

Toby welcomed Shari with a long embrace,
No words needed to be shared or spoken;
The tears streamed down two silent red faces:
It was a healing of the two hearts once broken.

Once again Toby was in physical therapy,
And he gave it his all every day;
Then a Doctor walked in from the NASA Space Center:
He said good news Toby; Things are coming your way.

We've developed a new kind of robotic limb,
That we'd like you to test. What you say?
It has a ball for a foot and a gyro for balance:
You can walk with it—Toby interrupted, OK!

Two weeks passed by, the gyro legs arrived,
A ball foot on a pole with a tether;
Toby tried them on, and the best part was:
These legs could withstand any weather.

Shari drove Toby to his home at the ranch,
Hawkeye Tack was a stop on the way;
Toby bought a new rope and a Stetson straw hat:
Roping practice now fulfilled each new day.

The new legs worked well, Toby even could run,
He could dance, skip, hop, and jump rope;
But something happened, one day, on his way to Shari's place:
That left Toby helpless, and alone with no hope.

Toby walked the long way to Shari's ranch,
Going through the forest and down the bluff to the bridge;
When his gyro legs harness wore thin and snapped:
As he was crossing Blue Paint's pasture ridge.

Toby fell down; his legs could not work,
To crawl that distance was an effort in vain;
His right arm was not broken, but swelled in sharp pain:
Toby guessed that it must be a sprain.

It just happened that Blue Paint was grazing nearby,
Today this distant grass tasted sweet;
Unusual it was that she should venture this way:
A chance of fate that she and Toby should meet.

Toby had no idea that this pasture was Shari's,
That she had rented it just for Blue Paint;
Toby would argue that this mare wasn't his:
Blue Paint is a scrub horse and her this just ain't!

Now this strange horse was Toby's only hope,
Blue Paint watchfully stayed near Toby's side;
Evening turned to night as the air took a chill:
Toby knew that this horse he must ride.

This horse is not tall, about thirteen hands,
Her coat is a bright blue roan Paint;
She's smart and sweet headed. Then Toby says to her:
I've never seen a color so quaint.

Coyotes begin to howl, nocturnes are on the prowl,
A quarter moon hangs low in the sky;
The cold makes Toby shiver, mosquitoes rally for a feast:
Blue Paint slumbers in the soft grass nearby.

Toby studies the mare, He has an idea,
But is distracted by the mare's color and form;
Blue Paint remembers Toby and those bottles of milk:
She remembers tasty treats of sweet corn.

This couldn't be the horse that Shari spoke of,
The one she wrote of in letters sent to Kuwait;
Toby rolls to her side, grasps her mane and hangs tight:
Blue Paint arises to a slow walking gate.

Blue Paint's careful steps, are ever so tender,
Picking out - her path through the dark;
Treading the trail she very well knew:
Her every step carefully placed in its mark.

Two coyotes get brave as they stalk the slow pair,
The path is now rocky and steep;
The mare ever conscious of her unsure mount:
Down homeward trail, she continues to creep.

Toby cannot see where this mare is going,
He just trusts and clings to her mane;
His balance is unsure, but Blue Paint gets him to Shari's:
Where a frantic Shari is going insane.

Oblivious to Shari's shouts of scolding relief,
Are Toby and Blue in extra - sensory communiqué;
Shari's scolding focuses into audible reality:
Where have you been Toby? It is now nearly day!

Through the faint early glow of the day's new birth of light,
Shari sees Toby's legs are to no avail;
Gently she helps Toby as he climbs to the ground:
Hand over hand he slides down Blue Paint's tail.

Blue Paint fidgets then turns to face Toby,
Her soft nose nuzzles Toby's now slobbered face;
Her warm breath she shares in union with Toby's:
Their spirits unite to a singular embrace.

Toby turns to Shari and expresses,
I guess I'd better find some new legs;
Then Toby finds himself seated at Shari's breakfast table:
With fresh coffee, hot biscuits, and creamed eggs.

Time marches on, it is now one week later,
Toby is roping on his new gyro stilts;
Confident that he is ready to swing sisal from Blue Paint:
Shari supports him though her confidence wilts.

The morning's sun crests over Leheigh's luscious hills,
Blue Paint is saddled, she's bridled, and cinched;
From a mounting block Toby swings himself aboard:
Blue Paint steps carefully and forward she inched.

Toby gets a feel for the saddle,
The experience is old yet now new;
To Toby these stirrups are mere extensions of waste:
His hands grip to the saddle like glue.

Blue Paint senses something is unusually wrong,
Her slowed walk stops near the mounting block;
Slowly Toby wiggles to dismount Blue Paint:
Then falls to the ground like a rock.

Blue paint nudges and nuzzles the fallen rider,
Toby's anger into rolling laughter subsides;
Like a little boy with his dog, they play in laughter:
We'll have to change some things, Toby decides.

Toby spent that day in the tack shop,
With his saddle in the harness horse vice;
These stirrups have to go they're useless to me:
Then Toby made a leather holster like device.

First Toby wrapped in leather,
A mid-size pork and bean can:
Then he fashioned until the gyro ball on his leg:
Fit snug; like a meatball in saran.

Pleased with the stirrups that he fashioned,
Toby cinched his saddle onto Blue Paint;
So they think that I'm going to give up on team roping:
Well I got news for those folks, "I ain't!"

Toby swung up in the saddle,
He placed a ball foot in each leather holster;
Proud of what he had done Toby said to Blue Paint:
"Ahh! A stirrup from which I can bolster!"

Next Toby unflailed his thirty foot rope,
Made a burn fit to each goat skin glove;
Then he dallied and tossed his rope in the air:
And thought, God this is the life that I love.

Toby started roping the bale wagon tongue,
Till he could looped it from full lope passing by;
His rope in full sync with Blue's gathering legs:
Getting a feel for when to let his rope fly.

They practiced for hours through the noon day sun,
Till days sun through yonder hills did subside;
The ritual continued days, until sure of himself:
Toby said, "We are ready!" "Let's ride!"

At the Audubon T-Bone, Toby met up with Greg,
Greg headed while Toby roped from the heel;
A perfect match for team roping, their timing just right:
For team roping they just had a feel.

Between roping practice, in that December's cold snow,
Shari and Toby married in the warmth of their love;
They settled on a small ranch by the Raccoon River:
They were a match made in Heaven above.

How quickly those days of winter passed,
Toby and Shari were so lost in each other;
Each day Shari worked, Toby practiced his roping:
Before long Shari would become a mother.

Toby and Greg made quite a team,
They won at every roping they should;
They roped county fairs, Lake City, and Dayton,
To say the least they were good.

The calf would escape with Greg in pursuit,
Three swings and the head he would steel;
Then a split second later was Toby and Blue Paint:
With a lasso on the calf's outstretched heel.

They went on to Freemont, Grand Island, and North Platt,
At Denver they continued to win;
Greg and Toby were a team, they practiced all winter:
At first spring's circuit they toured again.

They did well in Scottsbluff, in Sidney, and Kearney,
They won Aksarben, and KC, MO.
They won in Amarillo, In Dallas, and Houston:
They won in every place they would go.

Toby and Greg's roping had improved that year,
By fall their time was even better;
They roped in Cheyenne, then Dallas and Fort Worth:
Their each roping was a ditto to the letter.

Just how far would they go? Nobody could say,
Would they go to Cowboy Hall of Fame?
They had qualified now for the NFR:
But were still just ole cowboys the same.

They awakened one morning with their trailer in Vegas,
They had made it to the "Big" NFR!
Through the chew in his lip, Toby chuckled to Greg:
And who'd a thought we'd be a goin this far!

They spent that day mostly fidgeting,
They stewed fretting with their gear;
I guess the thought of The National Finals Rodeo:
Was working their innermost gut fear.

Yet! What should it matter if they'd win tonight?
Or miss a loop and go on to lose;
This venture was started as a rehab game:
I guess tonight's roping would choose.

Shari drove to Las Vegas for the championship,
She was proud of how her Toby could rope;
And Blue Paint was ready, she was in her prime:
The NFR was now a reachable hope.

The intestinal butterflies fell somewhere behind,
As they rode the Grand Entrance Parade;
Greg, Toby, and horses were ready for tonight:
Then the National Anthem played.

Greg and Toby are anxious at the starting gate,
Playing mental pictures of what each will do;
Blue Paints ears are back. Her legs ready to spring:
Upon the calf that the team will pursue.

Rehearsing their pattern occupies their mind,
While waiting turn at the starting gate;
"Swing one, swing two, throw your feel to the heel."
"Trust your header 'cause Greg won't be late,"

Tonight Blue Paint was wired to win,
She was edgy and soaked with sweat;
But Toby was confident she would do all right:
For never had she failed him yet.

Now in the starting gate behind her string,
Blue Paint posed to do her thing;
The blood vessels pulsed in the mare's blue ears:
She crouched ready, at any second to spring.

The other team ropers experienced bad timing,
There was a miss of a heel or a head;
We've got it now! That buckle is ours:
Was the message Greg's sharpened eyes read.

The drawn calf was strong with a good set of horns,
He was fast, he was testy and lean;
He was a mottled, dark gray, with a hump on his neck:
He had a grunt that made him sound real mean.

With the suddenness of lightning from the starting gate,
With a leap the gate string was torn;
But Greg was on him with three swings and a loop:
That reaped him a rope full of horn.

Like a flash from behind was Toby on Blue Paint,
With a leap, a swing one and swing two;
Out of quickness, in slow motion, Toby looped up the heels:
Blue Paint dropped. Past the calf Toby flew.

The little Blue Paint hit the ground with a thud,
She rolled in a loud squeal of pain;
Toby hit the dirt hard, with his wind knocked out:
All reality had become suddenly insane.

Blue paint quivered, in a muffled groan,
Her eyes glazed with her last breath of air;
Toby crawled to her and spoke with a lump in his voice:
Stroked Blue paint and thought life's so unfair.

A tilt bed winch truck backed up to Blue Paint,
A chain was hooked around Blue Paint's sweated neck;
But Toby decked the winch man, the driver and assistant:
Guess they thought they had met a train wreck.

Toby yanked a gate away from a chute,
He laid it next to his horse Little Blue;
"Would somebody help me lift her on to the truck?"
It's no more than for your horse I would do.

An arena of cowboys gathered at Blue Paint's side,
Rolled her up and on to the gate;
The cowboys lifted her gently upon the trucks bed;
Then through silent glances consoled Toby, their mate.

Cowboys and spectators bowed in silence,
While Toby drove that truck away;
He drove into the night heading back to his ranch:
Arriving home late afternoon the next day.

Greg and Shari and several of Toby's friends,
Followed Toby as he got home that day;
Nobody spoke through the sound of shovels digging:
In Blue Paint's memory the cowboys dug away.

A well meaning neighbor with a backhoe came by,
This grave was special; Toby would have his way;
With each shovel of dirt another memory laid aside:
The saddened neighbor slowly drifted away.

When the grave was finished, Toby bedded it with straw;
In deep straw Blue Paint now laid in rest;
Still wearing her saddle, fully bridled with loose reins:
Toby gently laid his rope on her breast.

"Hi Mommy! Your back! Grandpa told me a story,
Did you buy Lucky Charms and Ice cream?
The boy left with his mother, A nurse wheeled the old man:
To his room, to rest with his dreams.

Back in his room, resting in his bed,
Reminiscent of a plate on the wall;
On the plate was the picture of a pretty young bride:
And her man so proud and tall.

The old man's eyes strained to read the plate's engraving,
"Congratulations on fifty years of happy marriage;"
"Best wishes to Tobias and Shari."

Keep your rope coiled,
Cowboy Poet,
Ray Meyers

Contact author
Ray Meyers
or order more copies of this book at

TATE PUBLISHING, LLC

127 East Trade Center Terrace
Mustang, Oklahoma 73064

(888) 361 - 9473

Tate Publishing, LLC

www.tatepublishing.com